DO YOU MIND

IF I ASK YOU A QUESTION?

52 Cage-rattling Life Questions Worth Being Asked

QUIET NEVIN

"Learn from yesterday, live for today, hope for tomorrow.

The important thing is not to stop questioning."

■ ALBERT EINSTEIN

DEDICATION

This book is dedicated to all those who have continued to encourage me to share and publish my photos and writings. Your determination paid off and you must consider yourselves as contributors to this book.

Thank you also to my family, friends, and mentors, as well as all the complete strangers who have let me approach and journey with them for a little while and ask questions that were probably too personal and often none of my business. I have never been good at knowing if something was OK to ask, and I may have mistaken your graciousness as a form of encouragement. You truly did not seem to mind.

Thank you to my Editor, Dove Champagne. All my mistakes combined with the various forms of creative writing in this book must have been challenging. Still, you also took time to leave notes on what resonated for you.

Finally and most importantly, a profound thanks to my enabler husband, who has been the equipper through this journey—giving me every bit of equipment, opportunity, time, and encouragement to capture the world around me in images (my joy) and in language (my nemesis).

This book simply wouldn't BE without him.

TABLE OF CONTENTS

Introduction

This book is a body of water that you are standing beside and considering how to engage with it.

Perhaps your experience will be a sky-facing float where you are content to be borne on images and writings alone. Or perhaps you'll set out to explore the edges, jotting notes and sketching your findings.

Whatever your experience, the impact of this book depends on its gradual consumption. It's not a book meant to be devoured quickly in one sitting, hence why it spans the seasons. For each week of the year, you'll find an image, a writing, and a facing page with one cage-rattling life question and room for notes.

And if we were walking together, these are the kind of questions I'd like to ask you—if you didn't mind, of course. Questions that we should unabashedly be asking each other and ourselves.

At the bottom of the notes area for each week, I've left a clue to help you find the location where that week's picture was taken. If you're interested in taking a journey to the location where a picture was taken, see the what3words topic at the back of the book for instructions on how to use the clue.

When you are ready to start this book, I suggest flipping forward to the image and question for the season and week you find yourself in and starting the book there.

Chapter 1: Winter

Squeaking footfalls, snowy dunes; Posts encased, ice-clad runes.

Frozen floes 'round me spread, I soldier towards the pier ahead.

Scarf and breath violently twist, silvered from the icy mist.

I look aside my stumbling stride, aside the tracks that serve as guide

To glimpse a huddled form, a mass of bending reeds, of shoreline grass.

And as I pause the sun prevails and for a moment halts the gales.

Scattering diamonds across the snow, setting ice-tipped fronds aglow.

My camera click midst short-lived hush steals the gem-encrusted brush.

Happily off with captured loot, I swift rejoin my laboured route.

Do you think you are humble? Do others?

///celebrate.frolic.raiders

why, said lofty leaf

of its true purpose in life

replenish the soil

How much of what your detractors say about you is actually true?

_____
_____
_____
_____
_____
_____
_____
_____
_____
_____
_____
_____
_____
_____
_____
_____
_____
_____
_____
_____
_____
_____
_____
_____
_____
_____
_____

///cone.horses.cheering

I find, said the pond,

trees are best at reflecting

it's what makes them wise

What deeply held secret would you find relief in setting free?

_____
_____
_____
_____
_____
_____
_____
_____
_____
_____
_____
_____
_____
_____
_____
_____
_____
_____
_____
_____
_____
_____
_____
_____
_____
_____
_____

///smooth.leaves.reported

oh we laughed, we cried

we shared secrets of the heart

those birches and I

On what life goal do you alternate between hope and resignation?

_____

_____

_____

_____

_____

_____

_____

_____

_____

_____

_____

_____

_____

_____

_____

_____

_____

_____

_____

_____

_____

_____

_____

_____

_____

///sprinkle.edges.rust

With cold resolve, and face a-stone

We part time

alone

With determined gait

Not holding back to seal our fate

The cameras are on you-it's your 15 minutes of fame-what are you doing?

_____
_____
_____
_____
_____
_____
_____
_____
_____
_____
_____
_____
_____
_____
_____
_____
_____
_____
_____
_____
_____
_____
_____
_____
_____
_____
_____
_____

///plenty.exact.graceful

nature's signature

while so easily captured

can never be forged

Do you believe that there is something bigger than you watching you?

_____

_____

_____

_____

_____

_____

_____

_____

_____

_____

_____

_____

_____

_____

_____

_____

_____

_____

_____

_____

_____

_____

_____

_____

_____

_____

///players.verge.risk

oh parhelions

oh tight ring of sundogs bright

we laud your halo

Have you ever intentionally brought joy to someone you don't like?

Not today, little gremlins three;

You won't swap my joy for your misery.

If anything, you make me laugh

Waving whip and flail and crooked staff.

I won't let you in to trouble me,

Off, off with you, little gremlins three!

Why do clingy people need so much while others don't?

///highlander.falcons.positioned

we brushed but one time

yet you cannot let me go

since you are a burr

Are you a best friend to anyone? Did you choose them or they you?

_____
_____
_____
_____
_____
_____
_____
_____
_____
_____
_____
_____
_____
_____
_____
_____
_____
_____
_____
_____
_____
_____
_____
_____
_____
_____

///canned.teller.wickets

Yet while I pause the sun prevails,

And for a moment halts the gales,

Scattering diamonds across the snow,

setting ice-tipped fronds aglow.

Is your heart fertile ground for new relationships?

///selfishly.folded.slightly

on ev'ry wee farm

rains seasons of provision

hurled from the heavens

Pick a person in all of history to share a coffee or tea with. What will you discuss?

_____
_____
_____
_____
_____
_____
_____
_____
_____
_____
_____
_____
_____
_____
_____
_____
_____
_____
_____
_____
_____
_____
_____
_____
_____
_____
_____

///taxable.gown.metalwork

each day we lament

so little time together

my coffee and I

What is one truth about you that you wish people could see?

///brave.colder.shrimp

impressed, asked the tree

you should see what's underneath

I'm this, but with depth

What good changes have you initiated that will continue without you?

_____
_____
_____
_____
_____
_____
_____
_____
_____
_____
_____
_____
_____
_____
_____
_____
_____
_____
_____
_____
_____
_____
_____
_____
_____
_____

///cupcake.starter.measures

what sets us apart

is oft how we're seen, not are

– blessing and a curse

CHAPTER 2: SPRING

What a surprise when we unfurl shoots fresh with dew,

And hurl toward the skies pushing leaves and soil askew.

And I'll ask what we were, what color?

And you, you'll say: Amaranth-blue!

We'll task to resplendor while the dirt is tender and before it snows anew.

And we'll hope by luck to be plucked by a passer-by; picked and dried,

Rinsed clean of this muck, freed of the mire in which we're stuck.

But for now, we just hide-me, with you beside,

Roots crossed, entwined like vines below the frost-waiting,

Blue Amaranth-ing,

in the dark, until Spring.

What is the safest bed you've awoken in?

_____
_____
_____
_____
_____
_____
_____
_____
_____
_____
_____
_____
_____
_____
_____
_____
_____
_____
_____
_____
_____
_____
_____
_____
_____
_____
_____

///crusty.hurried.pistachio

I climbed a trail, and you the sky

To meet at water's edge;

You peered out from cloudy high

While I from dewy sedge.

'I haven't forgotten our meeting place!'

'Nor I', your shine replied.

We passed the hour of dawn's embrace

while the world slept on beside.

Do you require an apology to forgive?

///delighted.fundraising.sludge

wisdom to forgive

eclipsed by unwillingness

spring encased in ice

At what age did you learn to hurry?

///chefs.cobras.vipers

"I'm a journey guy," said the escargot

as he hurried past,

"When I take this tree at half past three,

I get there twice as fast!"

What gifts do you deny that you have?

_____
_____
_____
_____
_____
_____
_____
_____
_____
_____
_____
_____
_____
_____
_____
_____
_____
_____
_____
_____
_____
_____
_____
_____
_____
_____

///loaders.explain.foods

purple sandcherry

going about your flow'ring

blind to your beauty

What attracts you to others? What attracts them to you?

_____
_____
_____
_____
_____
_____
_____
_____
_____
_____
_____
_____
_____
_____
_____
_____
_____
_____
_____
_____
_____
_____
_____
_____
_____

///pressing.moth.sling

white winter canvas

scrubbed clean of all autumn's hues

how you drink Spring's dyes

How would you define a toxic relationship to someone who is in one?

_____
_____
_____
_____
_____
_____
_____
_____
_____
_____
_____
_____
_____
_____
_____
_____
_____
_____
_____
_____
_____
_____
_____
_____
_____
_____
_____

///upcoming.miracle.defeats

how do all birds know

what will kill or make them grow

what bird told them so

What do you do today that contributes nothing to your eighty-year-old self?

_____
_____
_____
_____
_____
_____
_____
_____
_____
_____
_____
_____
_____
_____
_____
_____
_____
_____
_____
_____
_____
_____
_____
_____
_____
_____
_____
_____
_____

///deadwood.cheery.harvester

Did you know that bees sleep

And learn while they dream?

These honey makers we keep

Are more apt than they seem.

Do you spend time in non-verbal thought?

///legs.ailing.sleepover

my mind is set free

when I don't have to find words

to share what I see

What comes after?

///pressing.vampire.shack

ephemeral bloom

I have frozen you in time

eternal frailty

If you could make it so, who would occupy the space beside you?

_____
_____
_____
_____
_____
_____
_____
_____
_____
_____
_____
_____
_____
_____
_____
_____
_____
_____
_____
_____
_____
_____
_____
_____
_____
_____

///ghostly.consonant.shackles

hang on to a friend

who suffers along with you

tempering the go

Do you consider that you will pass into obscurity one day?

_____
_____
_____
_____
_____
_____
_____
_____
_____
_____
_____
_____
_____
_____
_____
_____
_____
_____
_____
_____
_____
_____
_____
_____
_____

///swimming.telling.myself

In the field I spotted you, no taller than the rye;

I laid me flat to join your world and face you eye-to-eye.

I pondered your obscurity, as I took a look;

Wondering if your life would change—made famous by this book.

What childlike qualities are you glad you still possess?

_____
_____
_____
_____
_____
_____
_____
_____
_____
_____
_____
_____
_____
_____
_____
_____
_____
_____
_____
_____
_____
_____
_____
_____
_____
_____

///decamp.emotional.naps

the goal of a fruit

can be summed up in one word:

immortality

If you could speak to your child self through this portal, what would you say?

_____
_____
_____
_____
_____
_____
_____
_____
_____
_____
_____
_____
_____
_____
_____
_____
_____
_____
_____
_____
_____
_____
_____
_____

///tragedy.aged.dwarves

Apon that heath that bords the pond

A haunted portal stood;

Blithe to dole a glimpse beyond

That none described as good.

CHAPTER 3: SUMMER

Stunned by sound, I face the sky

Drinking in from where I lie

A hummingbird whizzes by

Sparrows, bees, a dragonfly

Swaying tree tops catch my eye

Do they conduct this lullaby?

Summer, how to quantify

The tonic that your sounds supply.

What fear, story, or trait are you hiding from others?

_____
_____
_____
_____
_____
_____
_____
_____
_____
_____
_____
_____
_____
_____
_____
_____
_____
_____
_____
_____
_____
_____
_____
_____
_____

///childbirth.affirmative.gong

you are truly free

when any place feels like home

and you call all friend

Lay back, stare up, breathe deep, let go—what tries to pull you from your peace?

_____
_____
_____
_____
_____
_____
_____
_____
_____
_____
_____
_____
_____
_____
_____
_____
_____
_____
_____
_____
_____
_____
_____
_____
_____

///bake.eaten.prayers

white jew'l of the pond

borrowed cloud from summer sky

who could guess your bite

What or who helps you see things in a completely different way?

Once a stealthy goshawk

Set down to watch me dream

As I drowsed upon the rocks

That edged the wand'ring stream

Is it possible never to lie? What about to yourself?

_____
_____
_____
_____
_____
_____
_____
_____
_____
_____
_____
_____
_____
_____
_____
_____
_____
_____
_____
_____
_____
_____
_____
_____
_____

///uppermost.disengaged.hamstrings

web of lies I spun

I didn't know you'd catch me

predator turned prey

In what ways are you rich? How do you share it?

///reappears.disruptive.yesterday

Some were given many,

Some were given few,

Some weren't given any—

Which one of these is you?

If you were to get help to fix just one thing, what would it be?

_____
_____
_____
_____
_____
_____
_____
_____
_____
_____
_____
_____
_____
_____
_____
_____
_____
_____
_____
_____
_____
_____
_____
_____

///cars.decant.manhole

cheery sunflower

scores more will spring from your face

optimism seeds

When are you a leader? When are you a follower?

_____
_____
_____
_____
_____
_____
_____
_____
_____
_____
_____
_____
_____
_____
_____
_____
_____
_____
_____
_____
_____
_____
_____
_____
_____
_____

///disobeying.chimp.sentencing

When I awoke, a butterfly

fluttered down from the sky.

It fast applied its regal powers

as it turned about the flowers.

Beguiled, I pledged my fealty

to that dainty monarchy.

In what way are you immortal?

///cannily.massive.dose

busy at your work

blind to those who wish you ill

true humility

What thoughts or beliefs imprison you? Are they true?

///buttered.unattached.juries

I had a thought

Of breaking free

But other thoughts

Kept the key

And so I stayed

Behind the bars

Longing gaze

Fixed on the stars

Have you ever nurtured someone while desperately needing it yourself?

_____
_____
_____
_____
_____
_____
_____
_____
_____
_____
_____
_____
_____
_____
_____
_____
_____
_____
_____
_____
_____
_____
_____
_____
_____

///waterfalls.implore.sunscreen

sometimes a blue sky

makes plans with an open sea

conspiring solace

Whose lives are you building into and influencing for good?

_____
_____
_____
_____
_____
_____
_____
_____
_____
_____
_____
_____
_____
_____
_____
_____
_____
_____
_____
_____
_____
_____
_____
_____
_____
_____
_____

///fascination.thrusters.minimum

I studied you, yet not your word;

It was your acts instead.

While I scarce recall a thing I heard

Your deeds stayed in my head.

What impression do you leave on the animals that see you?

_____
_____
_____
_____
_____
_____
_____
_____
_____
_____
_____
_____
_____
_____
_____
_____
_____
_____
_____
_____
_____
_____
_____
_____
_____
_____
_____

///moping.dishonesty.ovens

"Humans intrigue me.

I cannot tell them apart.

They all look alike!"

What are your achievements a reflection of?

_____
_____
_____
_____
_____
_____
_____
_____
_____
_____
_____
_____
_____
_____
_____
_____
_____
_____
_____
_____
_____
_____
_____
_____

///billionaire.brewers.marker

oh gentle tension

that cradles a fallen leaf

grace that keeps afloat

CHAPTER 4: FALL

We enjoy so little of depth;

constrained to periphery and angled aspect

that veil substance and place.

Yet what shape takes a tree below?

What swims and crawls and flies

In water, earth, and sky

That we know not and will never see?

We are uncertainly sure

that all that we see

Is all that's to be seen;

Content with mystery.

Have you ever asked a stranger something you wish a loved one would ask you?

_____
_____
_____
_____
_____
_____
_____
_____
_____
_____
_____
_____
_____
_____
_____
_____
_____
_____
_____
_____
_____
_____
_____
_____
_____
_____

///shuddering.underwear.commutes

so much lies submerged

hidden from those around us

the secret best parts

Do you think most people feel "different" and not well understood? Why?

_____
_____
_____
_____
_____
_____
_____
_____
_____
_____
_____
_____
_____
_____
_____
_____
_____
_____
_____
_____
_____
_____
_____
_____
_____

///unicorns.snacking.constrained

We spend so much of our time trying to be understood,

If only by ourselves.

What do you do to slow down time?

_____

_____

_____

_____

_____

_____

_____

_____

_____

_____

_____

_____

_____

_____

_____

_____

_____

_____

_____

_____

_____

_____

_____

_____

///winemaking.tequila.appraised

the sun calls in night

swaddling us in bands of gold

rays of lullaby

When you were little, what special abilities did you dream you had?

In stealth I crept in bold trespass

To reach the fabled lake of glass,

And edging light in gentle stride

By magic, gained the other side.

❦ 103 ❦

What will you do to propel the next generation?

///housework.conclusions.forged

everything you are

will give life to what will come

nothing will you keep

Where do you fit into diversity?

_____

_____

_____

_____

_____

_____

_____

_____

_____

_____

_____

_____

_____

_____

_____

_____

_____

_____

_____

_____

_____

_____

_____

_____

///pillows.discreetly.clotting

diversity turns

shifting with every season

impatient to change

What would the ideal place you would escape to look like?

_____
_____
_____
_____
_____
_____
_____
_____
_____
_____
_____
_____
_____
_____
_____
_____
_____
_____
_____
_____
_____
_____
_____
_____
_____
_____

///flirting.denim.blur

a castle, mere shack

on a tempestuous night

brief bastion of stone

Could you survive owning nothing? What would you do?

Poverty of spirit is the poorest of poor;

It is the emptiest of pockets we can know.

🌀 lll 🌀

Can you describe an obstacle you overcame by sheer resoluteness?

_____
_____
_____
_____
_____
_____
_____
_____
_____
_____
_____
_____
_____
_____
_____
_____
_____
_____
_____
_____
_____
_____
_____

///precarious.tonality.crystals

ask any sheer cliff

skittish cedars don't exist

they are resolute

Which mystery do you most want to solve?

_____
_____
_____
_____
_____
_____
_____
_____
_____
_____
_____
_____
_____
_____
_____
_____
_____
_____
_____
_____
_____
_____
_____
_____
_____
_____

///refreshing.ranges.waterline

We are uncertainly sure

that all that we see

is all that's to be seen;

Content with the mystery.

What did you create the last time you practiced your hobby?

_____
_____
_____
_____
_____
_____
_____
_____
_____
_____
_____
_____
_____
_____
_____
_____
_____
_____
_____
_____
_____
_____
_____
_____
_____
_____

///wimp.analyst.gymnastics

reflections are gifts

they give us twice the value

twice the chance to think

If you were to give away something valuable, what would it be and to whom?

_____

_____

_____

_____

_____

_____

_____

_____

_____

_____

_____

_____

_____

_____

_____

_____

_____

_____

_____

_____

_____

_____

_____

///upswept.wire.grills

The wee small hours, the tiny time,

Feeds the heart, gentles the mind.

What are you a part of that is also part of you?

_____
_____
_____
_____
_____
_____
_____
_____
_____
_____
_____
_____
_____
_____
_____
_____
_____
_____
_____
_____
_____
_____
_____
_____

///unreasonable.mallards.milling

In every tree a leaf; in every leaf a tree.

Use of what3words Locations

If you are interested in visiting the location of any of the photos in Do You Mind, then you can find the what3words location at the bottom of the photo's opposing page.

For those who are unfamiliar with what3words, it is an easy way to find and communicate precise map locations, especially in places without street addresses, like parks and beaches. Every 3-metre square you can find on any map has been assigned its own unique combination of three words: a what3words address. For example, the location of the Dawn photo is: ///crusty.hurried.pistachio.

In the electronic version of this book, you can click the what3words locations provided. If you are using a paper copy of this book, then visit the https://what3words.com website and enter the three words from the what3words location.

what3words

Made in the USA
Middletown, DE
24 May 2021